The Wounds Turn to Flowers

by
Nick B Scott

The contents of this work, including, but not limited to, the accuracy of events, people, and places depicted; opinions expressed; permission to use previously published materials included; and any advice given or actions advocated are solely the responsibility of the author, who assumes all liability for said work and indemnifies the publisher against any claims stemming from publication of the work.

All Rights Reserved
Copyright © 2022 by Nick B Scott

No part of this book may be reproduced or transmitted, downloaded, distributed, reverse engineered, or stored in or introduced into any information storage and retrieval system, in any form or by any means, including photocopying and recording, whether electronic or mechanical, now known or hereinafter invented without permission in writing from the publisher.

Dorrance Publishing Co
585 Alpha Drive
Pittsburgh, PA 15238
Visit our website at www.dorrancebookstore.com

ISBN: 979-8-8860-4054-8
eISBN: 979-8-8860-4955-8

Wounds Turn To Flowers

Somewhere in another world pain must be beautiful

Wounds once painful that held the odor of grief

must now hold the sweet aroma of a flower

And now our once shameful scars are outlined in flowers

as a result to the tears we've used to water

Now look at us!

We've manifested into a bouquet – a walking cliché to wake up

each morning and smell the roses.

I dedicate this book to everything that allowed this book to be.
I dedicate this book to everybody who was a part of the journey.
Thank you.

Stage 1: Seeds

The Search

I've been looking in mirrors for the spitting image.
I been in open fields searching for unanswered lingering questions.
I've been feeling growing pains that have forced me to
rearrange my morals.
Suns that I used to long for and stars that I used to chase -
flames have now become dull and left me dry
So I've been praying for rain lately
Something to wash away this crystal glass vase
that fell to pieces on my floors called gloom
This vase that couldn't be easily gathered
and swept away with a broom.
I've been to the end of the earths for the answers
Went to every corner in search of the cure
No form of religion would do
And the closest peace I've come to is
when I'm looking in the mirror staring back you.

Self-Assessment

You used to move that way
Before you let them teach you that mountains weren't movable
Before you let them put out your fire for fear that they would
choke from the smoke
A fire that was once used as a signal
Before you let them teach you it was okay to be in the wilderness
and be lost
Lifetimes upon lifetimes

Bright-eyed wanderer
Now looks down because sun hurts eyes
Big beautiful heart that beats
Beats to a different tempo now
A once sharp mind
Attached to a mild tongue
Is now in survival mode
Speaks hurricane and set multiple tsunamis
When wanting to be baptized
Body is now an art gallery displaying scars and hurts
That many will walk and gaze at in disbelief
Talk of how they used to know
And neglect the beauty that now resides

The Child You Used to Be

The child you used to be

The eyes you used to use

The heart that used to beat to a rhythm of innocence

Is still there on the inside of you buried

It's worth the digging

It can still be used

Soil Lesson

Flowers that bloom too soon

Don't last too long

Seldom plucked

Over shadowed by the deep roots of the others

Who rose in their time

Flowers that bloom too soon

Are equivalent to flowery wallpaper

Beautiful to look at

No fragrance

gods

They say we niggas walking 'round reckless

We just lower case gods searching for purpose

Trying to steady catch a glimpse of our reflections in a system

of smoke and mirror

Living life

Simply trying

Why does it feel like the magnifying glass stands between us

and the sons and daughters of Zion?

Why are we the only one feeling the scorch?

Don't they know that the fire that burns us

Only turns melanin to gold

It only toughens our soul

Don't think for a minute that we don't long to be soft at times

To experience a life promised to us by God to Abraham

Questions

When was the last time you heard the voice of thunder?

Sat down and listened to its blueprints like you used to do the rain

And execute it like lightning?

The Dangers of Desiring Love in Motion

The dangers of desiring constant motion with love

Rather it be falling in it

Or walking with caution

Is that we get used to the goings

The need of the constant reminder

We desire the feel of it

To hear its voice every second

This thought of love we've conjured up

Ends to constant road blocks while on the journey with love

Leaving us to become merely targets for lonely

Neglecting the very things we need

Because we haven't grasped the concept that love can also be still

Thorns

These thorns that have lied dormant under our skin

Now burn as they press through our flesh to seek out the most high

Seeking the most high for its next assignment

Knowing they'll bring more enlightenment in the end

Than the pain and testimonial scars we'll be ashamed of until

we've learned to wear them proudly

In the beginning

Cycles

It was like we were doing the rain dance and expecting

the sun to shine

Expecting religious traditions to kill Love again and instead of

blood from the moon, wanting wine.

How drunk could we be?

How drunk could we had been?

To expect these back door dark covered remedies to be the answers

our souls needed at night.

It wasn't until we recycled the cycles that were handed down to us

A cup too bitter to bear consciously

That we'd see these rules did not agree with our existence.

These rules were not made with just in mind.

These rules weren't meant for us to keep and that by upholding this

system, we'd fail at every turn.

We'd be running a losing race and constantly exhausted while our

souls would thirst and beg for rest.

I Hate Poems That Rhyme

I hate poems that rhyme too much

Words too manipulated to perfection to trust the Writer's heart

who wrote them

If poems are to run parallel to life,

do you mean to tell the audience that your life is perfect?

Does your life only consist of orange skies to look at

over white picket fences?

Where the animals talk and trees dance

And all the privileged characters live perfectly ever after?

That might be exactly what your glossy eyes see

when you look in the world as a Writer.

But reality is quite different.

Remember

Remember feeling tucked away?

Remembering trying to create beauty from dungeons

Designed to bury you?

Remember manipulating tools

Mistaking wisdom and fools

Allowing them to rip words from your mouth

To trap your being

Saying yes

Turns into I do's that made you wish you never did

Taking moments to look in the mirror tying to rearrange your features

Back to the place where you could remember who the fuck you

were before the circus came to town

Do you remember?

Yes?

Good. Keep that feeling.

It'll be used as a tool in futures to guide you and keep you

in your freedom.

Soon

Soon means nothing to a love waiting on the arrival of his lover to come home.

It means nothing to a heart waiting to be healed.

Soon means nothing to an innocent soul promised freedom yet greets days still in a hole

Truth of the matter is time doesn't care about the soon.

Soon has nothing to do with time

It's in comparison to you thinking you love with your heart rather than your mind.

The Remedy

He keeps forgetting to remember

The voice in his head that says

He'll never touch skies

The voice that desires to replace each piece of hello light

With the darkness of deep and eternal nights

Vows

Vows bent

Vows contorted by fantasy

Shoes too deep to ever stand in

Shoes too heavy to walk in or slide across the floors

If the wrong song plays the wrong tune

How must we dance?

If both performed practices of learned behavior

On Wrong Lane

Spoke foul with wrong sayings

Who gets the main role deemed righteous?

Surviving with the only tool ever known as victim

The Longing of Home

When across the world

And I'm alone

A long way from anything familiar

I long for the simple times

I long for home

Walls Grow Weary Too

How long does it take for the strongest wall to grow weary?

How many storms does it take to put a crack in the foundation?

Do people not believe that walls get tired of being leaned upon?

Do people not give thought that pillars get tired?

Who will cry out for the wall that allowed you to rest on it?

Who will be grateful enough to verbalize their appreciation to just

the one of four walls that held home

together?

The Fruit Left Behind

We're the pieces of fruit that stand alone.

We're the only ones where the fruit not falling too far from the tree

analogy doesn't apply.

It's like we were picked from the heavens and fell from the sky

Because fragile trees that bend in the

Winds were too comfortable swaying grounds with shallow roots

to cultivate us

The fruit that would be so forgiving and nurturing

To feed the unforgiving and the very ones who neglected

our presence

Our power to make even the most bitterness pieces of fruit

see its sweetness

And bloom in winter

Circumstances

The truth is that sometimes circumstances were embraced

Circumstances that weren't worth the first glance

Maybe

Maybe we are following the greatest commandment

Maybe that's not where the problem lies

Maybe the darkness is us

Maybe we don't love us as much as we say

Maybe we don't love us the right way

Maybe our standards of loving others stem from our standard of

how we love

Ourselves

Maybe the greatest commandment isn't the greatest after all.

Feelings

We were taught anger first

We were taught how to shy away from feeling fear

And to never shed a tear

How is one to know that they are the salt of the earth if they've

never

Tasted their own tears?

Hands

Hands were made to praise in a white picket fence

that frames a white house

Where don't you worry about a thing rings

when the freedom bell is struck

Sung from mouths that never knew labor nor frown

How sweet that life must've been!

How sweet the dream!

Only in dream

For I've seen hands do many things...

A Day at a Time

We've lost the exact count of the number of times we've been lost
Bought the tickets and paid the cost so to now we're broke
And with these broken pieces we ask where do we belong now

A moment of lifetimes too big to simply sweep away
Sweet sunrise rises just the same as it always has
Allowing us to escape the thoughts at night
That gathered on the wall opposite from the wall with the window
that welcomes the moon

Our center cries out what to do
What's the next space?

How do you deal with the brokenness while maintaining
and appreciating the new skin?
How do you cope with the heaviness of yesterdays
while progressing in the new now?

Both with generosity
Both with kindness
Both with love and appreciation
Both one day at a time

Gatekeeper

You left the gate open

Put discernment on the shelf

Changed your clothes

Wearing only your heart on your sleeve now

You took your eyes off the sparrow and let them trespass because

through your eyes

They were chosen

Fathers

When they ask me how I came to be this way

I respond:

My father's father

Was fathered by fathers

Who knew no boundary

Knew the secrets of their God

Knew the burden of the journey

Knew how important it was to keep going

Clothed in Sun

The smell of dried spit stains the skin long after its been wiped off

Vulgar words spill over like hot tea

Scorches the soul

How does one take these murals off?

How do you put on the glory and wear the sun after the curse has

been spoken

And the spirit has been broken?

Tell me.

I Prefer the Sun

I prefer the sun that shines like no tomorrow is coming

The clouds that come in like tides holding enough rain

to completely wash away yesterday

I don't want partly anything!

I'm not concerned with feet that never greet each other

One foot in

The other out

Dreams Call

Dreams call you like
Telephone ringing
Alarm clock blazing
And you be hittin' snooze buttons like you'll wake up later
Like the gift of a guaranteed later was promised
Even though we know time is of the essence
And putting off today will delay your time to come
We gamble

Leaves me with questions like
Whatever happened to those times where we would run to the edges of the field to see the vision to constantly greet the sun?
Stepping into realms where time and space stood still
Where the worries of the world held no weight to the glory
And it was understood we weren't the authors of the story

Destiny awaits with open arms for all to reach her
Just waiting on daughters and sons to tap conscience
to see the bigger picture
Because dreams aren't given to the dead
Only the living
And if you can see them still
You can be them still
But it starts with you answering the call

Stage 2: The Germination

There

A young man said, "I'm not happy with myself

and where I am right now.

Seems like I have so much that I desire to do

And I'll be waiting for the next lifetime to do it in

When will I get there?"

Elder turns to him

A man of few words spoke

"You let me know when you get there."

Canvas

Teach us the way you used to teach by the rivers

Rinse the brushes

Start fresh on a new canvas

Make the colors richer

Tell the story a bit deeper

Tell how we came to be

Every conversation our spirit had before conception

The Ground

Even the most scorched ground

A ground given little to no rain

Still has the voice to rejoice

These grounds are still hopeful and evermore inspired

To still exist

To be

Even with little to no rain

It's grounded in the truth that it has a place in this world

Not being acknowledge or being shined upon

But knowing no man can stand without it

It has learned that while even being stepped on

Its dust will still rise

Consequences

The consequences are endless to those who haven't taken

the first step

All the beautiful possibilities of what could be

Imagine the wonderful ground not yet toiled

That your soul could roam freely if you'd only take that first step

God Sent

There wasn't a star in sight
From the sky of night
Nothing to light the way
No path of fire to bring you to me
You found your way still
You were God sent

A gift of strength for us
For we would be the ones to lift the curses from a blood line
A bloodline that wasn't ours to begin with
You understood the depth of the need to change
To have to intentionally lose our mind to find the true source
You stayed close
You were God sent

Heart connections soothed the hard conversations
We learned the importance of our words
Our eyes full of tears
For once not from a place of hurt, but that of love
You were God sent

We needed all from you
And all we needed was everything you had to give

Living Words to Live in this World

Don't sign your name on lines you don't believe in
Be sure to sit in every emotion that comes from within
before you release
Because still waters still run deep

Remember it's okay to be woke but twice as important to rest
Do what feels like fire in your heart
Go against the grain if need be
Keep your yes and time intimate because you're never
on anybody else's

Remember from which you come
But soar to the ever heights that beckon your spirit

Keep in mind that losing can be a form of protection
And that the winnings come only after you're thankful
for the protection

Here and now is all you have
Do the will
Keep the charge

Love Has No Form of Fashion

Love is wet Georgia Red Clay caked under her nail beds
That's been soaked through her once sharp white laced gloves
Along with a white subtle dress smeared with progress
Both a gift from her Father

Love is white tux- a tux that slowly begins to fade to various shades of oranges and reds
As the hem of his garment greets his selfless ankles and feet -
Feet he's learned to stand and deliver on
A gift given to him by his Father

I was once told that love was once clean
Though no one I know can recall when such a Love existed-
Just words on a page from an unknown author who wrote
to the future unknown sons
In a book with no cover that read

"Before sweat met brow
Lust given life
Before dominion was given up for adoption
And heavens were tangible
Love was splendid"

Oh, Day

Oh, Day!

You fooled me again

Said that today you would be the day you'd bring him back again

But like the days before

You lie to me once more

And like a fool I wait on tomorrow

Time

They'll tell you to slow down and
Reveal the act of being patient
Even when the fire is on your trail

This act took time to petition for
It'll also take time to deliver

For there are two things we know about time itself
Time flies in the moments of joy
And only time can heal

After Here and Now

One day after here and now is no longer

You'll look back at your periods of loneliness and realize

That you were the fruit too ripe to eat in that season

Yet too beautiful to throw away in a lifetime

Hopefully then it'll all make sense

Change

Change has never rung a doorbell asking to be let in

Where ego and other emotions beg

Change will simply ask

"Do you want me?"

"Good. Come find me…"

Change wants to be sought after

It has to be desired above all emotions

And healing has to be the motive that hangs on the walls of your heart like a motif

It wants you to thirst for it

To hunger for it

Because evolving has and will kill you daily

This is necessary for all

But it's not for the faint

For only the willing will see the power in dissolving

from useless mindsets

To building who they are called to be

Developed

Developing doesn't take place in a well-lit room

Doesn't take place with an audience sitting and cheering

It cares less about the judgement that follows you or the words

that will proceed you

Long after the developing has been developed by the developer

Duality Pt. 2

The rest of our lives will be spent

Holding close and making it through each day with a smile

As we encounter love

While also healing from the love that broke us

Heart's Memory

A heart can hold a memory

Attached to other loves in another life

While loving in the now

Some may call the act selfish

But a heart doesn't know how to sacrifice

It doesn't know how to close the curtains

To block the revealing warm sun

Doesn't know how to stop giving to hands

That may never cease to reach out

It knows the wonderful colors that can shape and mold the most

formless situations in lives

The heart knows its power and isn't afraid to use it

To sometime stand on the power of its memory alone

And bring other lifeforms to it

Live and Live Again

Don't validate them with your fears.

Don't send them off into a world designed to make them disappear.

Don't give them broken pieces and make excuses

why what you've given them isn't whole.

Don't let them settle, but show them who they are through the eyes

of God.

Train them to run and fly.

To go against the grain and try.

These things aren't impossible, planters.

You do these things by simply letting them

Smile

Be angry

Cry

Question

Grieve

Absorb

Love

You do this by simply letting them live and live again.

Love More Than Mine

Is it only, "Let Love Win" when it comes from a place that's

deemed comfortable?

Saw right in the sight from the only pair of eyes ever used

Does your love love you more than mine?

Does your love protect and correct you more than mine?

Does your love show you separate skies than mine-

Skies full of stars that glow brighter than diamonds and pearls

Do you think my skies show me less?

Love has many attributes

We all take in and reflect

Though the love that has to be defended the most

Has a survival that the love misunderstood the least will never

quite understand

Mother

My mother's mother

Heart like velvet with tiny pieces of flint

Moved the unmovable

Related more to the heavenly

Than the adamo

No Adam was ever worth stopping the curious nature that ran deep

Given to her before she was given to her mother

Whose mother had a mother formed in the very likeness

Our Truths

Now that the skies are grey no more

No smoke

No mirror

And religion has been put into its proper place

We now step into the sun to absorb our truths

The Needs

Thankful for the relationships that can tell me when my hair is out of place -for the relationships that can tell me when I have a stain on my shirt, and when my shoes don't go with my outfit.

Praise God for the relationships that can tell me when

my spirit is distressed.

When my energy could be higher and when my ego is too loud.

Both relationships are needed.

The Process

I bathe before I write

A clean body evoking pure writings

And for that hour or so

I've abstained from all I've considered to be immoralities

Like being uninspired and hateful

At that space and time

My body has completely been overtaken by the source and

My spirit releases wisdom that even I at times can't comprehend

"The Secret of Newness"

Don't think for a moment

That these children-

Children who found light in the wilderness

Now sit and proclaim perfection

Even if it appears that they're new

I assure you it's from the inside out

They've learned the secret of taking the broken pieces

of themselves

And placing it back on them slightly shifted

With a perspective different than the days before

WE.

Who will hold these memories for us?

Who will remember the spells cast?

Who will we be waiting on to set us free?

We.

So powerful

Too powerful at times for our own good.

To be the captive of our very own being

To be the only rescuer of our own dreams

Your Father's Tears

Before your mother

Your father carried you

You soaked in his experience

Like rain on cotton

Maybe that's why the tears he didn't cry

You do.

The Ocean

Let the ocean applaud you

When the audience is no longer there

And the encore is over

For there's no stage grander than the sea

No stage that understands the depth of you

This is the very stage that blended with sky

Yet was humble enough to become one with floor

It's important to be at peace with the element that God hovered

over before our very existence

Existed

The ocean was made for casting cares

With the discernment and wisdom to know

What to allow to sink or float

Either way you'll never see them again

Stage 3: The Flowering

Nick B Scott

Crack in the Wall

A memory survives
A memory that is a killer
Left an ugly crack on the walls of my being
That I would walk by every day in the house of my life

This memory kept blinds closed
Misplaced the confidence
Placed black veils over the mirrors
Where the blinded soul roamed
And then time showed up
And soon Soon had come

Soon brought the kingdom
Washed walls white
Took veils off of mirrors that sparkled from the sun
That danced through the windows from blinds that acted as if they
had never known the word down

Now the halls rejoice in song
Mature stairwells creak and testify of the journey and goodness
This house has been changed
Changed but not unrecognizable

The crack still remains in the wall

We (Gift and Kingdoms)

There were nights that the thunders were no match to our cries.

Times where rains that hit the land were no match

for the tears we knew.

Before coming into the knowledge of legacy

We were all we had.

Before we believed in the unthinkable

We were the visions from the past

We became tangible!

Visions that spoke

Before we were given names!

Nobody knew.

Not even we.

That we'd take the gift and build our kingdoms.

Black Child Soul Child

Black child

Soul child

How high will you soar?

When the journey gets too tiresome to walk so

And you can no longer feel your soles?

Were you meant to befriend gravity forever?

Were you meant only to look up at the glorious skies?

To only ponder at what was lingering on the other side

While standing on the shoulders of giants from yesterday

Holding on to the promises of today?

You can't be fearful to be released, Child

When the releaser sets you free

When a Black Child's Soul Child

Yearns to simply be

All That Is Perfect

Don't chase the possibilities for the ending

Take it by the hand and follow to experience the feeling

Time knows there's no valid reason to rush

And love knows all that's perfect

Embers

Embers

Remember

Formation

Embers

Remember

They come from a body much greater

Embers have no fear in flight

When the petition to soar has been granted

By the wise one

An ember knows its power

Yet submits to the wind

Trusting it to place it where it's needed most

To set a new blaze

Evolve

Who he has been and who he is becoming wouldn't make sense

explained to some

The one full of explanations

The one who spent a lifetime and then some

Begging for validations like a vagabond holding an empty cup

Resulting in no change

This body has seen death come thru it countless times

The fragrance of morphing

The stanch of change

Now only the outlines of him remain

While the center contains…

Untitled

I want you to know that you were special

One on one times

You depositing wisdom

Gave birth to sight to eyes full of webs

That couldn't see that there was no other option than to seek out

the dream

You did more than speak to my potential

You watered.

For that I love you.

Stillness

If I look to be grateful of stillness

In a world going fast

It's because I know what it feels like to be dizzy

She

She couldn't metaphorically tell you how she came to be when her magic defies the very essence of time

Of course we know that caterpillars in time turn into butterflies

And seeds into amazing orchards of fruit that in time will be right for the picking

But she has been beautiful from the start

From her soul

It just took time for her heart to see it

Stone Fruit

We were colorful
Right for the picking
Skin glowed just enough to get their attention
Yet no heights for the picking

We were young
So full of laughter while safe and comforted in our trees
Looking at the world from a perspective that many couldn't

Constantly moving when the wind would sway
Hoping that that day would be the day that gravity would answer
the prayers
Prayers that were mixed with naïve and youth
We thought we were ready to fall

Grass looks so green from here!
Dirt looks so rich!
The crowns these people wore as they walk and lay at homes feet!
How glorious!

In due time we fell.

The Answer

Looking up at the skies after being told about the heavens

Expecting the answers to simply fall like fruit being defeated by gravity

The questions that you doubt you can't live without

Ultimately leading you to take shallow steps in the waters of life

Where does the universe go to seek the answer?

The most glorious and creative space known to man

What is the greater outsider than it?

None but one.

The Bridge

And now that it appears to be that every star that led us here has

been snatched away by God

The bridge we could clearly see at one point

The bridge that carried the wisdom while crossing that poured

from the heavens like hyssop

Is no longer

We sit straddled between the gift and emotions asking the skies

who will be next to guide us

Who will write the words needed for Souls to speak and keep

the boundaries between us and the systems?

Who will be brave enough to isolate themselves from their ego?

Sacrifice their life for the callings that's standing behind the veils

Who will be the next bridge for us to cross while making

way for the others?

The answers quite simple

We will.

The Dance

Bend me, oh God

Sway me between worlds

Share the secrets that will change perspective

Make this dance immortal

The End, The Beginning

Who should worry so much about the end

When time seems to repeat

We see the same sun burn

Same moon glow

Same infinite stars blaze

We experience one's soul protected by the same body

We feel the life longing connection through heart and mind

A connection that can never truly be broken

The Face of God

Wondering the face of God is quite simple

Trust your eyes that were God given for sight in this world

and the next

Trust your nose that was God given for the fragrance of truth

Trust your ears that were God given for the bells signaling

you to move forward

Trust your mouth that was God given to you to speak

in and out season your story

It begins with looking in the mirror and using each gift accordingly

Each face holds the God you so desperately seek for

The Goings Go

The goings go

The trials slow down

And love of life

Is always in between

The sticks that hurt

The stones they throw

Are the foundation to kingdoms

You'll soon see

The bold will fold

The meek will last

Yesterday's left in the past

And here and now

Will stare you in the face

Were all one

We feel it all

The fire burns in all of us

There's a place in the sun for everyone

The Long Way Home

Taking the long way home is needed sometimes

More time for insight

More time to be grateful

More time to study the rearview mirror until what you thought you

could never live without

Has slowly faded away and is no longer in sight.

TIME? TIME!

TIME? FOREVER FEELS LIKE FOREVER HERE
SMELLS LIKE INCENSE CALLED INNOCENCE AND SUNRISE
PRETTY WIDE BROWN EYES
WITH A SAFE SENSE OF ARTIFICIAL TIMING
PAYING NO MIND TO SUBTLE CHANGES
BECAUSE NOW AND THEN DOESN'T EXIST
UNTIL ONE DAY IT DOES…

TIME! WORLD SPINS FASTER THAN I CAN WALK
I SEE NO REASON FOR CASUAL GREETINGS MORPHING
INTO CORNER CONVERSATIONS
THAT LEAD ONLY TO WISHING WELLS
WHEN DREAMS HIT SLEEP LIKE NIAGRA FALLS
WOKE NOW
I SEE GUILT AND EMBARRASSMENT WHEN THE SUN
HITS JUST RIGHT
THE LONG ROAD AHEAD TO ACHIEVE HITS DIFFERENT
NOW
WASN'T ALWAYS LIKE THIS
UNTIL ONE DAY IT WAS…

To The Writers

To the writers that walk around quiet

Eyes ever so open like newborn

Just coming into sight

You walk around with the weight of a pad and pen

Like stones and percussion tools that were used in the days of old

No erasers

Etched in stones

Unapologetic trait shown

Because the words that were written were the words

that were given

Pocket Full of Hymns

We carry a pocket full of hymns

Preparing for the times

When we have to remember that the odds aren't so slim

That the sunlight isn't just a dimmed light in the corner

And that the dream weaver didn't make a mistake

These conjured up 8-bar counts

Too old to recollect the first time

The first count was counted

Keeps the kept

Warms the soul

Prepares strength just for the next step

Garments of Ready

When the end begins to mirror the beginning

And the souls work is just about complete with journey

I hope that you're dressed in the garments of ready

That your once full of life

Full of dreams and desires

Full of gifts and promises

Are no longer in you for only you to see

But that they're now out and about in the world

For all to feel

The most fulfilled life

Is dying empty

To have nothing in you at dusk

Just a hollow shell fully prepared to return to dust

Even the Giver

Even the Giver

The one deemed Holy

Who gives freely from a place of freedom

Doesn't simply give you the desires without seeing your work

Home

It's important for children to feel home

To be protected in fields of peace where fantasy can be plucked

Without those years kids like flowers will surely turn into newly

planted old hollow oak trees

Dead before death in a new world of adulthood.

I Pray You Speak

There will be times when there will be no perfect way to tell the truth

There will be no perfect day where the land is always sunny
No land where tears don't exist
There will be no amen corner that constantly play harps
No glory like white stallions pulling your
chariot to make a grand entrance.

Sometimes all you'll have is yourself.
And whether it comes out soft.
Whether it comes out violently or as loud as trumpets

I pray you speak.

Intentional

There is so much power in being intentional

It separates you from the ones that have the talent, but no direction

And from the compassionate who lack understanding.

Legacy

My mentor

Master of words

Spoke like water

Used words of fire

Was taught by his mentor who would go further than he

To place it on the ones that he would nurture and in time leave behind

Losses and Findings

When you were lost

You attracted the lost

Sobriety nowhere near

All senses clinging to fear

And you were comfortable in that state

It felt less dangerous with likeminded beings near

There was no cost to pay

When your circle was broken

But when found

And the sun came out in search of you

And you made the choice to step fully into it and gleam

You then were prepared to lose what you found in your time of loss

And ready to receive the reward of losing everything once found

Mastered Flying

Bloody knees are now in the distance

It's safe to say that we no longer crawl

No!

We don't crawl

Walk or even run anymore

We found strength

Gathered our once plucked wings together

Now we fly

My Regards, Child

Open your eyes now, child

See what was always there before you

See what you couldn't see before

Long hallways many doors

Discern earnestly now, child

Say goodbye with gladness

Birth from a place of sadness

And watch dreams grow that'll shake the very foundation

You were fearful to look at in the first place

Love is not a race

It's not something that should be put to the test

It shouldn't be proven

It just is

Receive every bit of this offering these souls give, child

And give some whenever you can

Nina 78 and I

Sitting in a warm room while Nina 78 holds a conversation

with me

Artist to artist we both reflect times of heartbreak

Trying to compare the ache it brings

Artist are supposed to be creative

Yet not creative enough to perfectly pinpoint pain

The closest thing we could come to was

A vase falling and hitting the floor

Being put back together again

He Learned To Love Himself

He learned to love himself by simply loving you

You who made the world turn

And taught him that grace could also be formed into his likeness

Paint Me a Picture

Paint me a picture only using your smile

Use your picture perfect bone structure

To change our frown

It's something about your energy that we feed off of

Gives the feeling the street feels before the summer rain

To many you're the peace we didn't know we needed

You saved us

Some thank you while others live for you

The savior that didn't have to die

But felt the pain all the same

Pressure

No box has ever been big enough to hold the real you

Your spirit and soul is not brittle in battle

you will not fold

Sure you've felt the pressure

And needed more times for lies to be told

Because you held the truths that

In this life positives and negatives are what move the room

Responsibility

Understand we could never right our wrongs

We understand that not everything is forgettable

So we write our wrongs with great hope-

That our scars will possibly reach the new souls after us

Pouring wisdom on their ignorance before the same errors occur

She

She can turn water to honey

Bring good fortune

Leave you rich

No money

She was taught well by the Elders

The bloodline that never knew of a pipedream

Who had the magic on the inside

The God power to turn nightmares and

Shadows that danced across the room

Into sweet dreams

She knows there more to life than what she can see

But also knows she stunning like Chaka Khan Sweet Thing

All the goodness comes from her

And all come from her

Speak To Us

Don't speak at us

At times it'll do no good to speak to us

But speak into us

Speak bold in the seasons and times that have been

Speak into the seasons to come

Let the words blow away the ashes from before

Ignite a new flame we need

Vitality

There are days that I walk into my closet and pull out my best outfit

There are days that I walk out of my closet wearing my emotions

As a Black Man

Both are vital

Untitled Beauty

To the religious

Who sit in glass houses and throw stones at a world

They're still a part of

A world they're still in

Will never grasp the simple beauty of it

Yet the children to come

Will learn to cry and smile at the world

The same way the sun shines

While it rains for us

Beautiful moments

The Workings

When I realized that everything worked together

I stopped trying to manipulate life and simply live it

The death enemies spoke

Was the dying daily I was praying for also

Thank you.

Gardens of Strength

Oh, Isaac!

Did you know what the world would come to?

Did you know the seeds you planted and left behind would bloom

in the coldest seasons so boldly?

Flowers that wouldn't be scorched by brutal suns

Wouldn't scatter in the winds

Seasons wouldn't threaten their survival

Hands and hearts couldn't destroy it

Isaac, you created gardens

Gardens of strength

That would make way for the grounds to produce

even more long after

Green thumb is no match for wisdom

No price to gather for a persevered soul

Who knows how to plant beings in such a soil

And diligently watch for us to grow

Second Chance Blooming

For those who were forced to bloom

Before the season

Second chances feel like swimming

Upstream.

Swim harder.

Resistant builds strength

The strength you didn't have before

Will be the strength you'll produce in the time to come

It's not about trying to get back to the exact spot -

That's impossible!

It's about using the muscles of faith that tells you

The second chance is possible